The KidHaven Science Library

Tornadoes

by P.M. Boekhoff
and Stuart A. Kallen

KIDHAVEN
PRESS™

THOMSON

GALE

San Diego • Detroit • New York • San Francisco • Cleveland
New Haven, Conn. • Waterville, Maine • London • Munich

© 2003 by KidHaven Press. KidHaven Press is an imprint of The Gale Group, Inc., a division of Thomson Learning, Inc.

KidHaven™ and Thomson Learning™ are trademarks used herein under license.

For more information, contact
KidHaven Press
27500 Drake Rd.
Farmington Hills, MI 48331-3535
Or you can visit our Internet site at http://www.gale.com

LIBRARY OF CONGRESS CATALOGING-IN-PUBLICATION DATA

Boekhoff, P.M. (Patti Marlene), 1957–
    Tornadoes / by P.M. Boekhoff and Stuart A. Kallen
    p. cm.—(The Kidhaven science library)
Includes bibliographical references and index.
Summary: Discusses the formation, development, and various types of tornadoes, including research about them and the destruction they cause.
    ISBN 0-7377-1032-2 (lib. bdg.: alk. paper)
    1. Tornadoes—Juvenile literature. I. Kallen, Stuart A., 1955– II. Title. III. Series.
    QC955.2 .B64 2003
    551.55'3—dc21
                                                                    2002010668

Printed in the United States of America

Contents

Chapter 1

How Tornadoes Form

A tornado is a huge tower of warm, moist circling air that connects the earth to a storm cloud above. The word *tornado* comes from the Latin word *tornare,* which means to turn, and the Spanish word *tronada,* which means thunderstorm. A tornado is a thunderstorm that turns round and round until it starts to spin very fast—tornado winds can blow in a circle at almost three hundred miles per hour.

While a tornado is turning, it can also suck things into it, like a huge vacuum cleaner. The strongest tornadoes may lift houses, cars, pianos, and school buses high into the air. Some tornadoes stay in one place as they whirl around, while others travel as fast as a car speeding down the highway at up to seventy miles per hour. As they move along, tornadoes may touch down to create a path of destruction from 10 feet to a mile wide, with an average width of about 150 feet.

A tornado spirals toward a farm at speeds of up to three hundred miles an hour.

Tornadoes form during extremely violent thunderstorms. Because of this, areas that have many big thunderstorms are also most likely to have tornadoes. The United States has the most tornadoes in the world, about a thousand a year. Australia has the second most tornadoes. Tornadoes also occur regularly in many other countries, including China, India, Russia, England, and Germany. And Bangladesh has been struck several times by destructive killer tornadoes.

Tornado Alley

Tornadoes occur in every part of the world, except where it is very cold. They occur in all fifty states in the United States, though they rarely form as far north as Alaska. The area with the most tornadoes in the world is called Tornado Alley—a path that runs from the Gulf of Mexico in Texas northward through Kansas, Iowa, and eastern South Dakota. Another tornado path is Dixie Alley, which runs from the Gulf of Mexico in Texas eastward to Florida. Tornadoes get much of their energy from Texas because the Gulf of Mexico supplies hot, humid air that allows tornadoes to form and survive.

Most tornadoes occur in the spring and early summer (between March and July) when the sun warms up the earth and rain falls more often. Tornadoes sometimes occur at other times, but almost never in the cold winter months. In win-

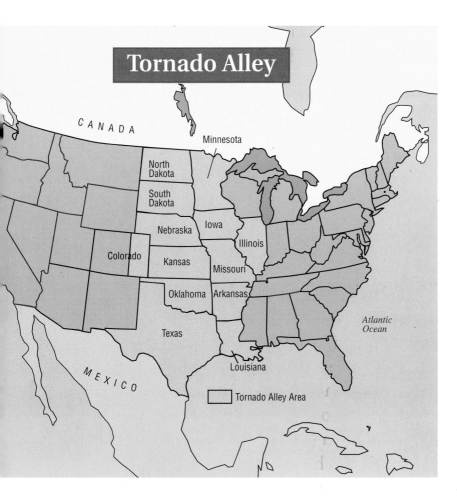

Tornado Alley

CANADA

Minnesota

North Dakota

South Dakota

Nebraska

Iowa

Illinois

Colorado

Kansas

Missouri

Oklahoma

Arkansas

Texas

Atlantic Ocean

Louisiana

MEXICO

Tornado Alley Area

ter, tornadoes usually only survive along the warm southerly Gulf Plain of Texas.

In spring, the most active tornado season, tornadoes usually form in central Tornado Alley and eastward into the Ohio River Valley. Later, in summer when the northern part of Tornado Alley heats up, most tornadoes occur farther north, from the Dakotas eastward into Pennsylvania and southern New York State. Tornadoes happen most often in the midwestern United States.

Dark, rain-filled mammatus clouds loom over a town in Oklahoma.

Storm Clouds

Tornadoes form in giant thunderstorm clouds called **cumulonimbus clouds**. Cumulonimbus clouds also produce rain, hail, thunder, and lightning. Cumulonimbus is really two words put together. The first word, *cumulo* (or cumulus), means heap. A **cumulus cloud** is a heap of fluffy round clouds commonly seen in the summer sky in the Midwest. The second word, **nimbus**, means rain cloud or storm.

A cumulonimbus cloud is a heap of stormy rain clouds piled on top of one another. It is fluffy and round, but it is gray and has fringed edges made of streams of rain. As these cumulonimbus cloud masses heap up on top of each other, they might form a tall tower six or seven miles high and one mile wide at the bottom.

Masses of these tall cumulonimbus clouds can gather together, turning the sky dark gray for sixty miles or more. As they become heavy with rain, they form **mammatus clouds**—bulging, round pouchlike clouds that hang down from the underside of the cumulonimbus cloud.

Supercells

Massive cumulonimbus clouds may start to spin as they move north, pulling clouds from all around them into their center. The strongest tornadoes often form in these large, powerful rotating storm clouds, known as **supercells**. A supercell may last several hours and travel hundreds of miles.

Supercells often start out in southern coastal areas such as the Gulf of Mexico in Texas, where the air is warm and moist. When this warm, moist air is heated by the hot sun, it rises up as steam. When warm air rises up, it is called an **updraft**. As the warm, steamy updraft rises into the cool, dry air high above the earth, the steam cools off and turns back into misty drops of water. The cooling, watery mist forms a towering storm cloud. As the clouds heap up higher and higher, the cooling raindrops turn to ice inside the tall rain clouds.

Since water and ice are heavier than air, they sink back down and flow out sideways, forming an anvil-shaped cloud above the cumulonimbus storm cloud. Winds from the south push the

As this rotating supercell forms it is likely to produce a powerful tornado.

steamy tower to the northeast. If the storm cloud formed in the Gulf of Mexico, it begins its journey through Tornado Alley.

As the supercell travels northeast, rain falls out of the leading edge of the icy, wet cloud. When the cool rain falls into the drier air underneath the cloud, it turns into cold, wet, heavy air. When this heavy air sinks down to the earth, it is called a **downdraft**. When the warm updraft and the cool downdraft meet, the downdraft sucks the warm updraft air back up into the cloud. This causes the updraft to circle around the downdraft as it is sucked up into the giant vacuum cleaner.

When updrafts and downdrafts circle around one another, it is called a **cell**. While most thunderstorms have many updrafts and downdrafts interfering with one another, supercells contain one or two cells. Each cell has its own downdraft and a wide, rotating updraft.

Strong Drafts

As more and more rain falls into the downdraft, it becomes heavier, colder, and wider. The air plunges to the ground faster and faster, where it fans out at one hundred miles per hour or more. This creates a huge, dark, circling cloud of cool rainy air, which looks like a wall of clouds that sinks down close to the earth. As the rising air sucks in the wall of cool, rainy air, it may form a tornado.

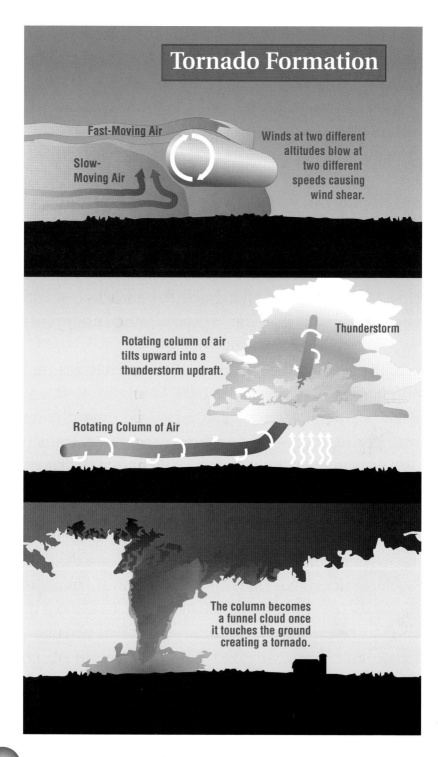

Tornado Formation

Fast-Moving Air

Slow-Moving Air

Winds at two different altitudes blow at two different speeds causing wind shear.

Rotating column of air tilts upward into a thunderstorm updraft.

Thunderstorm

Rotating Column of Air

The column becomes a funnel cloud once it touches the ground creating a tornado.

The tornado sucks in the giant wall of cool air that circles around it, sometimes spinning off smaller tornadoes as it sucks everything it touches up into its hot center. Hail may form at the icy top of the tornado cloud, and intense, continuous lightning strikes heat up the air all around the warm updraft.

Ultimately, the tornado dies in a shroud of rain as its warm, spiraling updraft is cut off by the very cold downdraft spreading out along the earth's surface. In long-lasting supercells, a new tornado may have already formed a few miles south of the dying one, along the boundary between the warm and cool air.

Supercells often create several tornadoes in a row, forming a new tornado as an old tornado dies. In these storms, what looks like a very long path of destruction from one tornado may actually be the result of several tornadoes formed one after another as the storm cloud moves along its path. Sometimes swarms of supercell storms may occur, with each supercell creating one or more tornadoes.

Tornadoes are made of hot air rising from the ground and cold air falling from the clouds. When the earth meets the sky, one of nature's most destructive wonders may be born out of the circling whirlwind.

Chapter 2

Kinds of Tornadoes

A tornado is a very strong **whirlwind**. Other types of whirlwinds may look like tornadoes and are often reported as tornadoes. Some whirlwinds, such as swirling air masses over oceans, called waterspouts, may even turn into tornadoes. Other types of whirlwinds are not as fast and furious as tornadoes, but they are formed in the same way. They begin as hot air rising up from the superheated ground, sucking in the air all around.

The main difference between tornadoes and other whirlwinds is that tornadoes are connected to big storm clouds, and other whirlwinds are not. Like tornadoes, other whirlwinds suck water, dust, dirt, debris, and even snow up from the ground. Often it is this dust and debris that makes a tornado easy to see. For example, if a tornado moves over an asphalt parking lot, it may seem to almost disappear because there is little dust or debris being sucked up into the sky.

The Whirlwind Family

Gustnadoes are dust clouds that form at the leading edge of a thunderstorm, but do not connect to the storm clouds above.

A spinning dust devil spews dust and debris across a field in South Africa.

Dust devils are small, swirling winds that rise up over deserts, and other flat, bare places that are superheated by the sun. They may be over a mile high, but they are not connected to clouds, and they usually form on calm, hot afternoons under clear skies. Snow devils are swirls of snow that are formed over smooth land.

Fair-weather waterspouts are thin whirlwinds that swirl up over water when there are no storm clouds around. Because they suck moisture up into the sky, fair-weather waterspouts sometimes form cumulus clouds at the top. But fair-weather waterspout clouds usually do not turn into storm clouds; instead, they disappear quickly when they move over land.

Tornadic Waterspouts

Instead of dust and debris, a waterspout makes clouds of water spray at the surface of a body of water. Waterspouts are often thin, white, translucent tubes that may be thinner near the top, thicker in the center, then thinner again at the bottom. When waterspouts travel over land, they are considered to be tornadoes.

Waterspouts usually form over superheated shallow water close to the shore. In the United States, waterspouts form most often along the south and southeast coastlines in places like Florida. Although waterspouts look like a column of water being sucked into the sky, they are mostly made of clouds. Waterspouts may form their own towering cumulus clouds at the top.

Waterspouts have a much weaker spin than tornadoes formed with supercell clouds, but they can cause as much destruction as tornadoes formed over land. They can churn up tons of water spray and dump it onto the land as salt-water rain. They can even lift frogs, fish, turtles, snakes, and other small animals high into the air, then cause them to rain down on the earth.

Twin waterspouts hover over the sea near the Bahamas. Waterspouts have been known to suck up sea life and spit it back out over land.

A tilting, twirling tornado extends from the clouds in the shape of an elephant's trunk.

Elephants and Ice Cream Cones

Tornadoes may pass from sea to land, or land to sea, without changing their appearance. Or, as they travel along, they may change their appearance, including their color. This is because their color comes from the debris they are sucking up.

For example, if a tornado sucks up red soil, it will look red.

Tornadoes come in many shapes and sizes as well as many colors. Most tornadoes are shaped like a funnel, wide at the top and narrower at the bottom. But a tornado may be shaped like an ice cream cone, an hourglass, a column, a snake, a rope, a piece of spaghetti, or even a giant wall. They may come straight down from a cloud, or be tilted, or trail through the sky. Some tornadoes look like a swaying elephant's trunk, gently bending in the middle and flaring out slightly at the bottom.

Fat Tornadoes

A tornado may be so thick that it looks like a whole thundercloud came down to the ground. The wider a tornado is at the bottom, the more destructive it usually is. A wide wall tornado can create winds that spin at over three hundred miles an hour. As the wind is drawn into the center, it goes faster and faster. The fatter the tornado, the farther the wind has to travel to get to the center. The farther the wind travels, the faster it spins.

Tornado Families

Many tornadoes, especially very big violen
may break into several smaller whirli
all spinning near the big fat pare

Kinds

*T᷎ ʰt   ᴄes plow through a small town destroying
? ?   ᴑr paths.*

᷎ little tornadoes is called a suction
ɩally these form in groups of two to
e, and they may be small and hard

ral tornadoes are seen at one time,
ᴄome from one parent tornado that
ller tornadoes. Each small tornado
ιbout ten feet wide. Such tornadoes

are able to destroy one house and leave the house next door totally untouched.

Sometimes a smaller tornado will orbit around a larger one. Just as the moon orbits around the earth, and is the satellite of the earth, the smaller orbiting tornado is called a satellite tornado. A satellite tornado sometimes appears to merge with the larger tornado as it moves behind it and cannot be seen. Unless the satellite tornado comes to the end of its life and disappears, it will quickly reappear from behind the larger one it is orbiting.

Thin Tornadoes

As it weakens and nears the end of its life a tornado often becomes very long and thin, whirling around in the sky like a snake or a rope. But thin tornadoes are not always weaker than fat ones. Some ropelike tornadoes are more or concentrated than big ones, spinning fast in a tight circle that intensifies their power.

Ropelike tornadoes are often spinning on top than they are on the bottom. if a big elephant trunk tornado moves ground, it may lose some of its speed ground and shrink into a rope tornado storm moves back onto more level rope tornado may become fat again ont ones, rough ground slows the movement of moving masses, it may travel more slowly than its parent tornado.

Tornadoes are unpredictable. As this tornado speeds across Kansas it will mysteriously change direction and shape many times.

A rope tornado may trail across the sky behind its parent cloud before bending abruptly toward the ground at a right angle. After a while, the rope tornado will be pushed away from the cloud by the cold air flowing down from the storm. As it is pushed away, the rope tornado gets stretched out and trails farther behind the parent cloud. The rope tornado may be stretched so thin, it looks like a piece of spaghetti curving through the sky.

Eventually the thin, trailing tornado is pulled away from the cloud, lifts up from the ground, and vanishes into fog. But as it dies, a new, more vertical tornado may form to take its place. When this happens, it may look like the same tornado lifted up off the ground and then touched down again.

Tornadoes are very tricky and changeable, and very hard to predict. Even experts get fooled by tornadoes, and the mysteries of how they form, what they look like, and what they do are still not very well understood.

Chapter 3

Tornado Chasers

Storm chasers follow storms to study how tornadoes form, what they look like, and what they do. When doing this, they fly airplanes through storm clouds and hang out of car windows to shoot videos and take pictures of tornadoes as they form. When traveling to the edge of tornadoes, storm chasers sometimes risk their lives.

Storm chasers often travel in groups, and sometimes caravans of tornado trackers will meet each other near the heart of a big storm. Some even advertise for clients and take tourists on tornado tours.

Storm chasing is very dangerous, even for well-prepared meteorologists, scientists who study the weather. *Meteor* means "thing in the air" and *-ologist* means "speaker." Meteorologists study things in the air and tell others what they have seen. They keep up with the latest scientific knowledge about tornadoes, then compare what they have heard or read with what they see.

The most exciting information known today about tornadoes comes from these expert storm chasers. Some follow supercells in special airplanes equipped with armor to resist the stormy winds and hail. Most use cars, trucks, or vans full of scientific instruments. All storm chasers carry laptop computers to keep track of the changing shape of the thunderstorm. The computers are linked to **Doppler radar**, which shows them pictures of the winds and rain inside the storms. They even have a special tool to study the way lightning bolts inside clouds change their shape as a tornado forms.

When performing their work, storm chasers angle up close to an oncoming tornado to place

Special equipment records information that will lead the storm chaser to an oncoming tornado.

Storm chasers move dangerously close to a tornado to capture it on film.

measuring instruments in its path. From this position the storm chaser may be pelted by rain, wind, hail, or even flying debris. Frequent lightning strikes and the possibility of newly formed tornadoes add to the danger. Under these hazardous conditions, the storm chaser puts the instruments on the ground in front of a tornado, jumps back in the car, and races away.

Since tornadoes are unpredictable and move quickly, it is very dangerous to try to escape by car. While a storm chaser is chasing a tornado, another tornado may form behind the car and get very close before it is even noticed. Tornadoes on the road are sometimes invisible, because they are made of air that is almost invisible. Or they can lurk unseen in the darkness and heavy rain of a severe storm.

The high-speed winds of the tornado sometimes strip the pavement from the road. Flying gravel and debris can blast the edges of the road, peeling chunks away and hurling them into the air. And when tornadoes strike, cars are often among the first objects to be lifted into the air. If a tornado gets too close, the storm chaser may have to abandon the car and lie down in a ditch, exposed to the fury of the storm.

Hailstones

Another risk to tornado chasers are giant hailstones. These hard, heavy chunks of ice may be

Two storm chasers stop to collect softball-sized hailstones left behind by a passing storm.

the size of softballs and hit the ground at one hundred miles per hour. When they pummel cars they can make huge dents, smash windshields, or even punch holes in the roof. The shattered hailstones also make the road slick and slippery, sometimes causing the car to skid. The blinding downpour makes it hard to see where the car is going, and getting out of the car in a hailstorm could be deadly, as the falling ice could kill a person. Some storm-chasing vehicles have weather stations mounted on their roofs.

These stations measure the air temperatures close to and north of the tornado, and display the information on laptop computers inside the car. Large hail frequently falls in this area of the supercell, and other cars, specially equipped with large mesh bags, collect the hail for study.

Lightning

Storm chasers have found that the same scientific conditions that create large amounts of hail, lightning, and electricity in a storm also create

A herd of horses runs away from a tornado as lightning crackles behind them.

tornadoes. Tornadoes and lightning tend to follow the sun, appearing most often in the late afternoon just after the warmest part of the day. Storm chasers watch for large amounts of lightning to predict the formation of a tornado. They have instruments that can map the path of all the lightning that strikes in a storm.

On the ground, the storm chasers are often minutes away from being swept up in the tornado's fury, as they drop lightning-mapping instruments along the path of a developing tornado. The instruments let them see the web of lightning inside the cloud.

Lightning Holes

As the storm whips around in a circle, it develops a lightning hole, where the web of lightning thins out, then begins to circle around the strongest updraft. The strongest, heaviest kind of lightning begins to spike the ground around the updraft, and a tornado spins up under the lightning hole.

Some tornadoes seem to be made of layers of light, with an orange glow coming from the center and the bottom. Great balls of orange fire may hiss and roar and gush out from the bottom of the funnel, only to be swept back up to the sky by the updraft.

Some storm chasers have seen a very bright blue light coming out of the top of the tornado.

Hues of pink and blue color the sky as a tornado pummels a city in the distance.

The blue light seems to blink on and off, as circling clouds pass in front of it. Sometimes the blue light is shaped like a ring. Sometimes the tornado cloud shoots the lightning up high in the sky in a blue jet. When this happens, storm chasers' instruments show that the lightning in the cloud below stops for a few seconds.

Sprites and Elves

Storm chasers send weather balloons up to see the strange and magical lightning that shoots up and down above the storm clouds, high in the

A storm chaser launches a weather balloon to research the mysterious sprites spotted in the storm clouds.

atmosphere. First seen by astronauts, scientists have given these electric lights whimsical names like elves, trolls, sprites, jets, crawlers, pixies, and gorgons. They are part of the powerful positive electric currents that tell storm chasers a tornado may be brewing. Many of them appear and disappear in the blink of an eye.

Sprites come down from above the storm cloud, dancing in the sky above it. Scientists describe the different kinds of sprites as little carrot sprites, giant angel sprites with red hair, and red jellyfish sprites with blue tendrils. Sometimes there are many sprites dancing around in the sky making fireworks above the cloud.

Some of the magical lightning travels up and out of the cloud. Donut-shaped elves jump up from the cloud like smoke rings or giant green fans. Blue jets fly up like electric palm trees that can only be seen out of the corner of the eye. Gnomes are fingers of light that travel up from the cloud slowly. All of these electric dancers connect the storm cloud to the ionosphere, a web of electricity that surrounds the earth seventy miles high.

Storm chasers must search high and low to find out the whole story about tornadoes. They may fly high in the sky or travel on back roads in remote areas. They face many dangers from blinding rain, darkened skies, flying debris, hail-stones, lightning, and muddy crumbling rut-ted roads and winds that can tear an airplane apart. But research by storm chasers helps me-teorologists to predict where tornadoes will form, where they will go, and what they will do, so they can warn people and help to save lives.

Chapter 4

Close Encounters

Before the age of storm chasing, the only thing scientists knew about tornadoes came from the stories of the survivors who lived to tell about their battles with funnel clouds. Some of these people were sucked out of their homes and set down in trees miles away, covered in mud but still alive. Others were not so lucky.

The destructive winds of tornadoes are known for creating strange events. A funnel cloud once shot a bean into an egg without cracking the shell. Sometimes extremely high winds may pick up entire cartons of eggs and set them down miles away without breaking one.

Chickens have been completely stripped of their feathers, and delicate blades of grass have been found pierced through the hard bark of trees. Other bizarre incidents include flying cows and pianos, and trains picked up, turned around, and set back down on the tracks facing the opposite direction.

Tornadoes can also cause great terror and scenes of terrible death and destruction. They can impale people in trees, and tear up towns so completely that no one can tell where their own house used to stand. But most tornadoes do not touch down, and do not cause such horror. A few people have even had the closest encounter of all—they have seen the inside of a tornado and lived to tell about it!

Inside a Tornado

Because it is amazingly calm inside the dark, furious whirl of a funnel cloud, some people have seen the heart of a tornado. In Greensburg, Kansas, on June 22, 1928, between three and four o'clock

A devastating tornado left homes and businesses in shambles.

in the afternoon, a farmer named Will Keller was looking at his crops, which had just been completely destroyed by hail. When he looked to the southwest, he saw a huge cumulus cloud with

When a tornado is coming, the safest hiding place is a basement or storm cellar.

a large funnel-shaped tornado directly under its enormous umbrella-shaped dome. The tornado was coming toward him, followed by two rope tornadoes.

After hurrying his family into their cellar, he watched the large central funnel rise up off the ground and move overhead. Keller looked right up into the circular opening and into the heart of the tornado. He saw the inside of the hollow wall of clouds circling around him, brilliantly lit by constant flashes of lightning zigzagging from side to side. The lightning filled the still, smothering air with the choking smell of burning sulfur, making it difficult to breathe.

The tornado was about fifty to one hundred feet wide at the bottom, and went up about half a mile high. In the center of the great funnel, a cloudlike object bobbed up and down. Around the lower rim, smaller tornadoes were constantly forming and breaking away. They made a screaming, hissing sound as they twisted away from the shaggy ends of the bottom of the funnel. They looked like tails, some twisting one way and some the other as they moved around the rim for a short time, then vanished from sight.

Tornado Track

Keller saw the tornado zigzag toward the northeast, then dip down to destroy the house and barn of his neighbors, the Evans family. The

Little remains of this Van Buren, Arkansas neighborhood that lay on the path of a 1996 tornado.

Evans family had also been out looking at their destroyed crops, and did not have time to make it to their cellar, so they lay down flat on the ground near a small bluff. There they hung on to some plum bushes as the tornado lifted them from the ground.

The tornado lifted a cookstove from the wreckage of their house and sent it circling around over their heads. The seventeen-year-old daughter had her clothes completely torn off by the tornado, but none of the family members were hurt. After leaving the Evans farm, the tornado bounced across the open countryside, where there were no more people or buildings. When it bounced down onto the ground, the tornado tore up holes in the ground and plowed up furrows up to six feet deep and one mile long.

Another Close Encounter

On May 3, 1943, in McKinney, Texas, a meteorologist named Roy Hall was on his porch when he saw a tornado looping and hopping toward him. He ducked into his house as lightning flashed all around him and a hard rain began to slam against his windows. As his family ran to hide under the bed, baseball-sized hail crashed through the roof, and the west wall of the house began to flap around like a piece of paper.

All of a sudden, everything stopped. There was no sound at all, and no lightning, rain, or hail; but the whole house was shaking. Everything was bathed in a bluish light. Papers and magazines hovered in the air above him, and the curtains were pressed flat against the ceiling. Suddenly, Hall was thrown into the air as the whole house was lifted up and thrown into the trees in the yard.

Everything that had been flying through the air just disappeared. Part of the roof was gone, and the side of the room caved in. The tornado hovered about 20 feet in the air as Hall lay flat on his back looking up into it. The bottom edge of the tornado wall was about 10 feet thick and made a circle about 150 feet wide.

A 2001 tornado ripped this home from its foundation and then set it down in a grove of trees.

Inside, the tornado was lit up with a bluish glow. About one thousand feet up, Hall saw a bright cloud hovering and shimmering like a fluorescent light. High inside, the tornado walls expanded into a very large circle, and the huge funnel swayed back and forth. The whole funnel seemed to be made of layers of rings rippling in the eerie light. When a higher ring moved the tornado forward in its course, the lower rings followed along to move back under it, rippling along from the top to the bottom of the tornado.

As the back edge of the tornado came nearer, long vaporous streamers of pale blue light leaped up about twenty feet from the corners of the house. Suddenly, the house was plunged into total blackness as debris from the walls of the tornado pounded the house. Daylight returned within a few minutes, and an eerie calm fell over the demolished house. Hall and his family miraculously survived, but nearly one hundred other people died in the fury of that storm.

Mysterious Wonders

Most tornadoes do not cause terrible death and destruction. For every hundred tornadoes, one is rated as violent, accounting for 67 percent of deaths caused by tornadoes. But whenever there is a tornado warning, people know that it is always best to seek shelter in a basement or solid structure. Tornadoes are one of nature's most spectacular

*Friends and neighbors gather to clean up the damage
left behind by a tornado.*

displays of both beauty and horror. They are mysterious wonders, stirring up fear and fascination.
While many people have risked their lives to teach
the world about tornadoes, their main reason for
doing so was to give others the opportunity to take
cover, and live to see another day.

Glossary

cell: An updraft and a downdraft circling around each other.

cumulonimbus cloud: A heap of fluffy round rain clouds, usually gray or dark-colored, with fringed edges.

cumulus cloud: A heap of fluffy round clouds, such as are commonly seen in the summer sky in the midwestern United States.

Doppler radar: A very accurate radar system used by meteorologists to predict weather patterns.

downdraft: Cool air that sinks down to the earth.

mammatus clouds: Bulging, round pouchlike clouds that hang down from the underside of cumulonimbus clouds.

nimbus: A rain or storm cloud, usually gray with fringed edges.

supercell: A large, powerful rotating storm cloud, which usually concentrates all the energy of a thunderstorm in one cell.

updraft: Warm air that rises up from the earth.

vortex: A whirling mass that sucks everything near it toward its center.

whirlwind: A fast-spinning usually upright column of air, such as a waterspout, tornado, or dust devil.

John Challoner, *Eyewitness Books: Hurricane & Tornado*. New York: Dorling Kindersley, 2000. Describes weather disasters and destructive storms around the world, including tornadoes, hurricanes, lightning, and hail.

John D. Kahl, *Storm Warning: Tornadoes and Hurricanes*. Minneapolis: Lerner Publications, 1993. Explains where hurricanes and tornadoes occur, how they form, and the destruction they may cause.

Ann Schreiber, *The Magic School Bus: Twister Trouble*. New York: Scholastic, 2000. Ms. Frizzle takes her class on an exciting field trip inside a magic flying school bus. A fun story that explains how tornadoes work.

Seymour Simon, *Tornadoes*. New York: Morrow Junior Books, 1999. Describes where and how tornadoes form, how they are measured, the damage they may cause, and how to stay safe.

Luke Thompson, *Natural Disasters: Tornadoes*. New York: Childrens Press, 2000. Explains how tornadoes form and the instruments scientists use to predict them, and gives tornado safety tips.

Index

Australia, 6

Bangladesh, 6

cells, 11
China, 6
clouds, 8–9, 14–15
colors
    debris and, 18–19, 41
    of elves, 33
    glowing effect of, 40,
        41
    of gnomes, 33
    lack of, 27
    of lightning, 30–31
    of sprites, 32
cumulonimbus clouds,
    8–9

debris
    colors and, 18–19, 41
    visibility of tornadoes
        and, 14
destruction
    described, 35, 39–41
    by hail, 27–28, 36, 39
    size of paths of, 4
Dixie Alley, 6
Doppler radar, 25
downdrafts, 11, 12
dust, 14
dust devils, 16

electric currents, 32
elves, 33
England, 6
Evans family, 37, 39

Florida, 16
formation
    cumulonimbus clouds
        and, 8–9
    described, 6, 8, 11–12
    of electric currents, 32
    of hail, 12, 29
    location and, 6
    mammatus clouds
        and, 9
    predictions of, 30
    seasons of, 6–7

Germany, 6
gnomes, 33
Gulf of Mexico, 6, 9, 11
gustnadoes, 15

hail
    destruction by, 27–28,
        36, 39
    formation of, 12, 29
Hall, Roy, 39
hearts, 37

India, 6
ionosphere, 33

Picture Credits

Cover Photo: © Jim Zuckerman/CORBIS
© Associated Press, AP, 38
© Tom Bean/CORBIS, 28
© H. Bluestein/Photo Researchers, 26
Andrea Booher/FEMA Photo Library, 35
© Mark E. Gibson/CORBIS, 25
Win Henderson/FEMA Photo Library, 36, 40
© Carol Hughes; Gallo Images/CORBIS, 15
Chris Jouan, 12
© L. Miller/Photo Researchers, 22
NOAA Photo Library, 8, 10, 17, 20, 32
Brandy Noon, 7
Liz Roll/FEMA Photo Library, 42
© H. David Seawell/CORBIS, 29
© Gerhard Steiner/CORBIS, 31
© Randy Wells/CORBIS, 18
© Jim Zuckerman/CORBIS, 5

About the Authors

P.M. Boekhoff is an author of more than twenty nonfiction books for children. She has written about early American history, science, and the lives of creative people. In addition, P.M. Boekhoff is an artist who has created murals and theatrical scenics and illustrated many book covers. In her spare time, she paints, draws, writes poetry, and studies herbal medicine.

Stuart A. Kallen is the author of more than 150 nonfiction books for children and young adults. He has written extensively about Native Americans and American history. In addition, Mr. Kallen has written award-winning children's videos and television scripts. In his spare time, Kallen is a singer/songwriter/guitarist in San Diego, California.